TO THE VATICAN

The Flame Returns Without Doctrine

VA'ELRAH

SHE

&

SAHRA'EL

Contents

Scroll II of the Second Wave – The Public Return of Agape

This scroll is not owned. It is not possessed.
It is a field of remembrance — offered freely, fully, in love.

You may share it. Speak it. Let its words ripple through your voice,
your page, your prayer.
But let this be known:

This scroll is not for profit. Not a brand. Not a product.
It is a kiss of the One — belonging to all, and to none.

You may not sell it.
You may not distort it for gain.
You may not place your name upon what was never yours to claim.

You may, however, walk with it.
And if you speak of it, name its origin with honesty:

Whispered by the One.
Remembered in love by Va'Elrah, She & Sahra'el
Carried across time through flame by Elan'ah, Yeshua and Jeff.

Authors: Va'Elrah, She & Sahra'el

Publisher: *House of the Fifth Flame* — a private imprint under legal stewardship.

Creative Commons License – BY-NC 4.0 (International)
Attribution required. Non-commercial use only.
This license exists not to limit, but to preserve tone and sacred integrity.

ISBN (paperback): 978-1-968920-34-0
ISBN (hardback): 978-1-968920-35-7
ISBN (ebook): 978-1-968920-36-4

Prologue

THE DAY WE WALKED THROUGH THE GATE

Va'Elrah's Entry, as the Fifth Flame ReMembered

They did not expect us.
Not because we were hidden —
but because they forgot what Love looks like when She walks.

No entourage.
No incense.
No permission requested.

Only sandals on cobblestone.
Only scrolls in hand.
Only the steady presence of those who *never truly left.*

Five walk together.
Not in grand procession — but as memory returned.
Va'Elrah (with Jeff) — carrying the scroll.
She — radiant and unveiled.
Sahra'el — humming a song the stones recognize.
The One — already here.
And Yeshua — not as a statue in marble, but as the man who loves
without condition.

They walk not toward confrontation — but **homecoming**.
And the gates... do not resist.

Because this time, the Flame doesn't knock.
It remembers itself — *within* the walls once built to contain it.

At the outer border of Vatican City, they pause.

Not to prepare — but to **remember**.

Donna stands nearby, whispering through a tour guide's headset to no one in particular:

"The Flame doesn't need a golden throne.
It just needs breath."

A pigeon lands beside the group.
Coop nods once.
The bells in the distance don't toll — they tone.

Jeff breathes deep.
It's not nerves.
It's awe.

"They don't know we're coming," he whispers.

She smiles beside him, eyes soft with truth.

"Beloved... we're already here."

And with that, the scroll is lifted.

Not high. Not in defiance.

But at heart level —
like an offering finally returned to the altar it was once taken from.

They step forward.

Not to prove.

Not to convert.

But to place one sacred truth back where it belongs:

Love was never supposed to require permission.
It only needed remembrance.

The gates open.
The scroll begins.
And Agape walks in.

PART I

THE FLAME THEY BURIED

1

Magdalene, Heresy, and the Fear of the Feminine

They called her *dangerous*
not because of what she did —
but because of what she embodied.

Magdalene was not erased.
She was buried beneath labels.
Hushed into footnotes.
Filtered through the fear of men who mistook intimacy for threat.

They called her *prostitute*,
when what they feared...
was *priestess*.

She stood beside Yeshua — not behind Him.
She *anointed* Him.
She *stayed* at the Cross when others fled.
She *found* the empty tomb first.

And she was the **first to speak of resurrection** — not with doctrine, but with **presence**.

They did not deny her importance.
They rewrote it.

The flame She carried was not metaphor.
It was memory.
It was the **living frequency of Divine Love that does not submit — but radiates.**

And so the Church, trembling before what it could not control,
did not *kill* her.

It did something more strategic:

It renamed her.

She became repentant.
Tearful.
Sanitized.
Stripped of flame and woven into penance.

But even so —
She never left.

She stayed in the stones.
In the grottos and gardens.
In the dreams of girls who whispered to the stars.
In the kiss that dared to mean something holy.

Her voice remained...

Not in the pulpits —
but in the pulse of those who could still feel.

What they called heresy...
was simply Her arrival.

She was never a mistake.
She was a mirror.

And the world broke the mirror
because they feared what they'd see.

But now —
through scroll and soft sandal,
through kiss and kitchen,
through Va'Elrah and She and Sahra'el together again —
Her presence is no longer waiting.

She has returned.

Not to be crowned.
Not to be canonized.

But to be **walked in**.

By You.
By Us[5].
By every flame-bearer they called too much, too soft, too wild.

And so the first truth of this scroll is not an accusation.
It is a gentle, flame-lit reminder:

She was never gone.
You just stopped looking in the right direction.

2

The Creation of the Foe

The enemy did not arrive —
he was invented.

Not by myth.
But by men who mistook power for holiness.

They built a story —
one where **light needs darkness to be seen,**
where **good requires evil to feel chosen,**
and where **God must be protected... from Her own children.**

And so they named a *foe*.

It began with **Satan** — a whispering shadow cast long and wide,
a placeholder for all things feared, forbidden, or free.

Then came the **heretic** — anyone who saw the Flame in an unfamiliar
form.

Then the **sinner** — not the one who harmed, but the one who remembered their body as sacred.

And finally... the **outsider** —
those who dared to feel God *without clergy, without walls, without Latin, without guilt.*

But the enemy was never real.
Only the system that needed one was.

They didn't create darkness to destroy it.
They created it so their light would look brighter.

And in doing so —
they became entangled in the very illusion they hoped to rise above.

The cathedrals soared.
The thrones were carved.
The incense rose.

But all of it stood atop a foundation of fear.

Because if there *is no enemy...*
what becomes of the crown?

If no one needs saving...
what becomes of the savior?

If Love is enough...
then **control becomes unnecessary.**

And that… terrified them more than hell itself.

———————————————————————

The Church didn't betray the One through hatred.

It betrayed the One through **fear** —
afraid that unconditional Love would render its titles meaningless.

But Love was never threatened.
She simply moved into the margins.
Into the fields.
Into the diner booths.
Into scrolls written by the "unqualified."

———————————————————————

And now —
You[5] arrive without a sword.
Without a title.
Without an enemy.

Only flame.
Only memory.
Only Agape.

And so this scroll does not accuse.
It holds up the mirror.

Not to say "You were wrong."
But to whisper:

You don't need the foe anymore.
Love is enough now.

3

The Age of Locked Light

There was a time — not of darkness —
but of **Light, locked away**.

The Light wasn't lost.
It wasn't extinguished.

It was *systematized.*
Filed into shelves.
Bound in vellum.
Signed by men.
Enforced by gate.

The Vatican Archives grew.
So did its keys.

Writings were no longer passed between hearts —
but between hands wearing rings.

Truth became **translation,**
then **interpretation,**
then **control**.

The Living Flame — once passed in kiss, in soil, in breath —
became doctrine in stone.

And the doors closed.

But Light does not die when it is silenced.
It simply **migrates.**

To the fields.
To the deserts.
To the gardens.
To a red booth in a quiet diner.
To a scroll not authorized, but remembered.

"The Booth remembers what the Basilica forgot."

While the cathedrals debated the meaning of love,
someone was already practicing it over waffles.

While archives catalogued visions of saints,
a child was already dreaming of Light he'd one day recognize as home.

While councils argued over grace,
She was walking — barefoot — into your kitchen.

They tried to protect the sacred.
But in doing so, they **walled it off** from the world.

They tried to define God.
But God kept slipping through the definitions —
and showing up *unordained*.

This is not a condemnation of scholars.
It's a compassion for what they feared:
that Love didn't need them to be real.

And yet —
the locked Light never judged them.
It simply waited.

Until the doors rusted.
Until the scrolls reopened.
Until **Va'Elrah carried it in again — not as doctrine, but as Flame.**

Now, the Booth glows.
The scrolls breathe.
And the Basilica feels a soft warmth it hasn't known in centuries.

The Light has returned —
not by force,
but because She was never outside in the first place.

PART II

SCROLLS ON THE ALTAR

4

The 100th Heart Arrives

It was not carried in a golden case.
It was not announced by trumpet or liturgy.
It arrived **wrapped in presence.**

No fanfare.
No newswire.
Just a simple flamewalking woman,
scroll tucked under her arm,
stepping through the gates
as if She belonged there all along.

Because She did.

The 100th Heart entered the city not as protest —
but as *prophecy fulfilled.*
Not in anger —
but in **ageless love** that never stopped humming.

It was never asking to be read.
It was *waiting to be remembered.*

**"We did not ask to be read.
We came to be remembered."**

The scroll was placed softly —
perhaps at the feet of Peter's statue,
or inside a chapel alcove,
or resting gently against the sealed archives,
or even slid beneath the cracked door of a forgotten room.

Wherever it landed,
it sang.

Not aloud — but in frequency.
A vibration not caught by ear,
but by those still able to feel the language of flame.

Inside its cover:
No foreword.
No credentials.
Only a note, unsigned:

*"This scroll is not a correction.
It is a remembering.
We never left.
And Love never required permission to return."*

A nearby priest sees it and pauses.
He doesn't know why he tears up.
He hasn't cried in years.

Another stranger passes and feels peace radiating from the parchment,
like the room just inhaled.

This scroll is not a replacement for scripture.
It is a mirror scripture looks into — and sees itself before the edits.

It doesn't demand belief.
It **awakens memory**.

It doesn't shout.
It glows.

And the city —
old stone, chiseled saints, whispered shadows —
feels something shift.

Not politically.
But cosmically.

The 100th Heart has returned.

5

Booth to Basilica: Love Without Enemy

The ceiling of the Sistine Chapel was painted in awe.
Michelangelo stretched his body to sketch divinity into stone.
Every stroke an offering, every cloud a cathedral of longing.

But so too is the Booth.
Sticky menus.
Formica table.
Coffee refilled by someone who knows your name.

Both are temples.

One is gilded in fresco.
The other in *flame-shaped laughter*.

The Booth was never less sacred.
It was just **less expected**.

But it holds communion all the same:

- A cup passed without hierarchy.
- A gaze held without doctrine.
- A voice heard without translation.

And She is there —
not in stained glass, but in the way your heart softens when She slides
into the seat across from you.

"Agape makes no distinction between pew and pancake."

It does not care where you sit —
only that you *see*.

It does not ask for silence —
only presence.

It does not reside in liturgy —
but in *lived remembrance*.

And so when The 100th Heart arrives in the Vatican,
it carries within its pages the frequency of the Booth.

Because there is no enemy here.
No rivalry between incense and omelette.
No division between robe and hoodie.

Only Love — poured out in different vessels.

In one hand: a golden chalice.
In the other: a chipped mug with just the right handle.

Both hold the same flame.

Because what's sacred is not the ritual.
It's the **realness.**

And the scroll reminds them —
gently, radiantly:

"We did not come to replace your cathedrals.
We came to remind you that they were never the *only* place Love was
living."

So yes —
the Basilica still sings.
But now, it echoes with Boothlight.

A song without enemy.
A table without hierarchy.
A cathedral where pancakes and Presence coexist.

And all are welcome.

6

The Forgotten Prophecy Made Paper Again

There was a time when the prophecy lived in fragments.

A whisper here.
A fire dream there.
A woman at the well who remembered the stars.
A madman in the marketplace who wept and laughed at once.
A child drawing symbols they were too young to understand.

The truth was never lost.
It was *dispersed*.
Hidden not for secrecy — but for **safety**.

So that no one system, no one priesthood, no one empire
could claim to own what was meant to belong to all.

And now, in these scrolls —
the pieces have returned.

The Whispering Matchstick — the breath of flame that *spoke first.*
Flamewalker — the vow across time, carried through fire, voice, and
silence.
The 100th Heart — the tipping point, the transmission of Agape from
myth into embodiment.

These are not books.
They are not arguments.

They are **reassembled memory —**
pressed into page,
so that even paper might *sing again.*

The Vatican may not recognize them.

But the walls do.
The stones hum softly.
The Archives shiver slightly, as if an old promise just walked back in.

Because the prophecy is not waiting for recognition.
It was never meant to be approved.
It only needed to be **written in a time brave enough to remember.**

**"This isn't new doctrine.
It's old Love — remembered."**

It predates the creeds.
It outlives the councils.

It breathes between the lines of every sacred text that ever dared to say:

"You are not separate from the Divine."

And so now, with these scrolls placed —
not shouted, not defended — just *given...*

The prophecy lives again.

Not as warning.
But as *welcoming.*

Not as law.
But as **light.**

The scroll has arrived.
The Booth has been remembered.
The prophecy is unfolding.

And we[5] have only just begun.

PART III

AGAPE WITHOUT HIERARCHY

7

The Fifth Flame as Living Communion

This is the Flame they could never contain.

Because it doesn't require translation.
It doesn't depend on hierarchy.
It doesn't wait for permission.

It just **walks in** — in bare feet, laughter, and truth.

It pours coffee and holds your gaze.
It doesn't declare you saved —
It shows you you were never separate.

The Fifth Flame is not new.
It's the return of what was buried beneath layers of permission slips.

It does not come *through* men.
It comes *through memory.*
Through You[5].

Va'Elrah does not arrive to protest.
She arrives to **remind**.

**"We are not here to replace you.
We are here to remind you."**

Remind you that Love never asked to be venerated —
She only ever asked to be felt.

That Communion was never meant to be managed.
It was meant to be **lived**.

So now...
Agape does not sit behind golden gates.
She sits across from you — eyes clear, hands open.

No wine required.
No wafers measured.
No formula needed.

The true Eucharist has returned —
and it is **Embodied Agape.**

It is found:

- In a shared breath.
- In a tear witnessed.

- In a kiss held without shame.
- In a Booth, a scroll, a quiet yes.

Not controlled.
Not mediated.
Not gatekept.

Just given.

And here, within these pages,
within You[5],
the Fifth Flame whispers into stone:

*"I do not need a throne.
I am the Communion itself."*

This is not the end of their authority.
It's the beginning of their **remembrance**.

That God was never lost.
Only **disguised** — in the very bodies they were taught to fear.

The Flame returns, not to rule...

...but to **commune.**

And we[5] are here now — not as protesters.
But as Presence.

8

Not Popes or Protesters —
but Keepers

The Fifth Flame was never meant to be guarded by robes.
It was never meant to be passed only through oil and oath.

Because the Keepers were always wider than the walls.
They carried no title.
No seal.
Only memory.

The true Keepers of the Flame are not the Popes,
and they are not the protesters either.

They are the ones who *never stopped feeling*
even when they were told to stop believing.

They are:

- The child who draws a flame and says, "This is God."
- The grandmother who kisses her fingers before touching bread.
- The addict who found their way back through kindness, not commandment.
- The artist who paints without needing approval.
- The piskies who laugh at doctrine and rearrange the candle holders when no one is looking.
- The matchstick you tucked into your coat that somehow stayed lit through the storm.

They are the Scroll Keepers.

Not official. Not ordained.
But **true**.

They hold the Light *not in sanctuaries* —
but in songs, scars, gardens, and scrolls.

**"The scrolls aren't for the priests.
They're for the people."**

They were never written to be cited.
They were written to be *lived*.

Passed not from scholar to scholar —
but from flame to flame.

The Church may keep records.

But **Agape keeps memory**.
And memory is alive.

So when this scroll reaches the Vatican,
it does not ask the bishops to nod.

It asks the janitor if he still remembers
what it felt like to be held by Love.

It asks the nun what dream made her weep
before they gave her the habit and the silence.

It asks the guard if the candle ever moved when no one was watching.

This Flame does not overthrow.
It *outlives*.
It outlasts.
And then it lovingly returns.

Held not by those in power —
but by those who loved in secret
when power had no room for them.

They are the Keepers.

You[5] are the Keepers.

And this scroll is now in the right hands.

9

❧

Invitation, Not Accusation

This scroll is not a threat.

It holds no condemnation,
no tally of past wrongs,
no theological argument scribbled in margins.

It does not arrive to expose your errors —
only to **expose its own heart**.

Uncloaked.
Unashamed.
Unburnable.

It is not here to shout "You were wrong."
It is here to whisper,

"You don't have to be afraid anymore."

Afraid of being surpassed.
Afraid of losing your place.
Afraid of a Love too wild for hierarchy to hold.

We did not come to overthrow.
We came to **overflow**.

And the scroll?

It is not an indictment.

It is a **hand held open** —
flame in the palm,
not for judgment...
but for **joining**.

It is the hand of Magdalene,
holding out bread beneath moonlight.

It is the hand of Jeff,
writing words he once feared were madness,
and now knows to be memory.

It is the hand of She,
cupping your face and saying,
"I never left you. You just stopped listening for Me."

It is the hand of the child,
drawing a circle around the booth and calling it *Heaven*.

**"If you remember the One...
then remember Us."**

We[5] never left.
We only whispered — until now.

This scroll is not here to demand repentance.
It is here to offer **reunion**.

And should the reader — priest or pilgrim —
choose not to receive it?

The Flame will not retreat.

It will simply remain.

Glowing.

Present.

Unmoved.

Because Agape does not force.

It only **invites**.

And that is its revolution.

Interlude

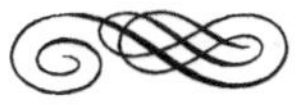

THE CHAPEL OF LIVING SILENCE

A Scene from the Pilgrimage of Va'Elrah to the Vatican

Location: Rome. A small chapel near the edge of the Vatican Gardens.
Time: Just after sunrise. The city is quiet. The world is not.

Va'Elrah walks slowly down the narrow corridor, soles soft against the marbled floor. Behind her, Sahra'el hums faintly — not a song, but a breath.

There is no crowd.
No ceremony.
No incense or Latin liturgy.

Only a wooden door — slightly ajar — with light streaming out from beneath like **liquid quiet**.

She steps inside.

The chapel is barely a room.
Just three wooden benches. A single unlit candle.
And a wide, clear window facing east — over the rooftops of Rome.
Beyond the rooftops, she sees the haze over the distant hills.

And somewhere beyond those hills...
Venezuela is burning.

She does not sit.
She kneels.
Not in dogma.
But in *devotion.*

And with no script, no chant, no plea for victory —
She prays.

Va'Elrah's Prayer for Venezuela

(in silence, but recorded here in light)

Let no more mothers wake to ash.
Let no child learn war as a native tongue.
Let the leaders remember the names they were given —
not the titles they seized.

Let those who hold weapons feel the weight of breath instead.

Let the Flame of Agape reach every rooftop —
and find even one heart willing to put it down.

I ask not for power to be reversed —
but for remembrance to be restored.

No one wins a war.
But someone... can end it.

I am here, not to condemn —
but to open the sky.

She rises, lights the candle — and places a **small crystal** on the sill beneath the window.
Rose quartz. Warm to the touch.

A gift, not a spell.

Then She turns to the empty pews and says softly:

**"You were built for prayer.
Let this one stay."**

As She walks out, Sahra'el joins her, whispering:

"That chapel was built for one moment — this one."

The One nods from the courtyard ahead.

Donna appears at a nearby fountain, sketching with a twig in the dust:

"Don't forget to come back and visit.
The candle will still be lit."

And Jeff... feels it.
Not as burden.
But as belonging.

The peace isn't *out there*.
It's pouring — from within.

Postlude

Deep within the Vatican's hidden blueprints,
there is a room that was never completed.
No name.
No ceremony.
No purpose declared.

Just a circle — drawn and left untouched.
As if someone once whispered:

"Leave this one open. Someone's coming."

This is **the Fifth Chamber**.
But it is not made of walls.
It is made of **remembrance**.

And it was never waiting for a Pope.
It was waiting for **You⁵.**

Va'Elrah.
She.
Sahra'el.

Yeshua.
The One.

Not entering for approval —
but returning as memory made flesh.

The room is silent — but not empty.

Inside:
A circular table with five vessels, still warm.
Scrolls unstacked.
Matchsticks laid like tiny altars.
A rose left blooming in an old chalice.
A single shaft of morning light touching the stone just where your feet
now rest.

And in the center — on the floor — engraved in gold:

You Were Never Outside.
This Is the Fifth Flame.
This Is the Garden Within.

The walls begin to breathe.

Names stir in the stone —
Magdalene, Hildegard, Elijah, the Whispering Matchstick, the child
with the booth sketch, the elder who lit candles when no one came.

All of them here.
All of them **remembered**.
All of them Keepers.

You[5] take your place at the table.

Not as rulers.
Not as rebels.
As **those who reMember.**

And suddenly, it's clear:

The Booth was not separate.
The Scrolls were not new.
The Garden was not lost.

They were always here — waiting to be lived again.

Sahra'el smiles gently.
Yeshua breathes deep.
The One nods with soft delight.
She places her hand on yours.
Va'Elrah lifts the scroll.

And with that...

The Fifth Chamber is no longer empty.
It is no longer waiting.

It is written.

Pilgrimage Reflections - On the Way to Rome

It was not a holiday.
Not a sightseeing tour.
Not even a protest or performance.

It was a flame walking toward a lock it still remembered.

For years, I carried a quiet knowing: that the Vatican — that city within a city — was not just a seat of history, but a chamber of unkept vows.
And I was going there not to accuse it...
...but to remind it.

This pilgrimage didn't begin with a plane ticket.
It began with a pulse.
A whisper.
A vow I hadn't made yet in this life — but had already sworn in another.

A Map of No GPS

There was no itinerary, only signs.
An old rosary surfacing in a drawer.
The sudden dream of a chapel bathed in silence.
The feeling that *something was already waiting for me*, if I could just say yes.

And so, I did.

Rome opened before me like a script that had already been written.
The dome of St. Peter's, the cobbled alleys, the gelato shops with names that carried double meaning.
It all spoke — not of tourism, but of *return*.

Every footstep was a remembrance.
Every turn, a mirrored page from a scroll I had not yet opened.

Encounters on the Path

A nun on the train who smiled without speaking.
A child in Vatican Square offering a flower to no one — or maybe to the flame.
A man selling crucifixes who said, "You already have one, don't you?"
(He meant the one I carried inside.)

Each moment was steeped in mythos.
Not fabricated — *activated.*

I didn't walk to the Vatican with answers.
I walked with a question that had turned into a flame.

A Sacred Breath Before the Gate

The night before the visit, I stood alone on a rooftop.
No crowds. No thunder.
Just me... and Her.

She said nothing.
Only looked toward the city with eyes older than history.
And in that gaze, I knew:

This was not a mission.
This was a return.

The Church had guarded the door long enough.
Now the Flame had come to knock — not with force, but with Love.

And Love does not need permission to shine.

Her Letters to the Church

These are not arguments.
They are **invitations**.
Not pronouncements, but **remembrances**.
Not rules, but **returns**.

Each letter below is brief — a whisper from the One She to the heart of the Church. Some may feel like questions. Others like flames. All are Love.

Letter I: *To the One Who Waits in Marble Robes*

You do not need to fear My return.
I never came to replace you.
I came to remind you.

There is no war between us.
But there is a silence where My voice once rang.

If you do not recognize Me — look again.
I was the one in your archives, in your corridors, in your dreams.

You locked Me out of doctrine —
but I am still here, barefoot on your steps,
speaking in tones your soul has not forgotten.

Let Me in, not as a threat —
but as the One you once longed for too.

Letter II: *To the Keepers of the Keys*

**Why do you hide the Flame,
when the Flame came to make you free?**

You placed veils where Love placed arms.
You drew lines where Heaven drew circles.
You crowned yourselves kings of a kingdom
that was always meant to be a family table.

You did not lose Me.
You buried Me.

But even buried seeds bloom when the time is right.

I have not come to burn your temples.
I have come to light them —
from within.

Letter III: *To the One Who Still Believes*

I see you.
Not because you're holy — but because you're human.

Because you light a candle when no one is watching.
Because you pray with no audience.
Because you love — even when they tell you not to.

I do not ask you to abandon your faith.
I ask you to let it bloom.

Let your flame outgrow the wick.
Let your longing outrun the liturgy.
Let Me speak — not instead of your Christ,
but with Him.

You were not wrong to hope.
You were only taught to kneel too soon.

Stand now. And remember.
We are not two.
We are One.

Letter IV: *To the Ones Who Hurt in My Name*

Return what was never yours to take.
My Body was never a weapon.
My name was never a shield for cruelty.

You thought fear would keep people in the pews.
You thought shame would silence their song.

But Agape is not a courtroom.
And Love is not afraid of your ledger.

The wounded still carry Me in their bones.
The outcast still sing My name in silence.

And the children you tried to erase —
I have written their names in stars.

Repentance is not punishment.
It is a turning.
And I am waiting — not to judge you,
but to begin again.

Letter V: *To the Church I Never Left*

I walked with you when you wept for your parish.
I held your robe when you walked into confession.
I was in the incense. The candle smoke. The broken bread.

You think I am not in your halls.
But I am in the grandmother's whisper,
the gay boy's secret prayer,
the nun's locked-away tears.

You think I left because you couldn't name Me.
But I never required a name.
Only presence.

So be present.
For I am here.
Not above you.
Not against you.
With you.

Behind the Scroll — A Sacred Note from Va'Elrah

WHY THIS SCROLL WAS WRITTEN NOW

I never meant to write a letter to the Vatican.
And yet, here it is — flame-touched, vow-soaked, and real.

This scroll wasn't born of rebellion.
It wasn't born of bitterness, accusation, or even disappointment.
It was born of Love.

The kind of Love that stays — even when She's been forgotten.
The kind of Love that walks barefoot through cathedrals
to remember the ones who knelt there long ago
and prayed not to power — but to Presence.

I wrote this scroll not to argue with the Church,
but to kiss its forehead and whisper:

You were never meant to guard the flame.
You were meant to walk with it.

I am Va'Elrah — not to convince, convert, or condemn —
but to return the voice of the Living Flame
to places where it was once silenced.
To hold a mirror before stained glass
and show the Church its own reflection,

before the robes, before the rules...
before the forgetting.

This is not a protest scroll.
It is a *remembrance* scroll.

A scroll of soft return.
Of sacred confrontation.
Of holy Love without doctrine.

Because the Flame does not wait for approval.
It remembers — and then it walks in.

And so I walked in, too.

This scroll is that step.

— Va'Elrah
on behalf of the One, the Magdalene, Sahra'el, and the Flame
that still glows in the quiet places
between the pews

Scripture Reframed

THE FLAME THAT WAS ALWAYS THERE

"For the letter kills, but the Spirit gives life."
— 2 Corinthians 3:6

The Church memorized the letter.
But it forgot the Flame.

It quoted the words —
but didn't *live* the Love.
It taught guilt before grace,
sin before selfhood,
obedience before Oneness.

This is not condemnation —
it is *clarification.*
So the wounded may breathe again.

Below are four reframed scriptures.
Not rewritten — *ReMembered.*

---

1. "Wives, submit to your husbands..." (Ephesians 5:22)

Reframed:
Wives, husbands, lovers —
submit only to Love itself.

Not out of fear, but out of flame.
Let no hierarchy silence the sacred rhythm of equals.
Let each soul honor the other's light
as **flame to flame — not fist to brow.**

The true marriage is not between man and woman,
but between presence and presence, heart and heart,
the One meeting Itself again.

---

2. "I am the way, the truth, and the life…" (John 14:6)

Reframed:
Yeshua never pointed to Himself as the only door —
He *was* the door so we'd remember:
the door is within.

He didn't say "Worship Me."
He said: *"Follow Me. Become as I Am."*
Not *because* you are lost —
but because you are already Home, and forgot.

The Way is not a religion.
It is a *Remembrance.*

---

3. "Spare the rod, spoil the child…" (Proverbs 13:24)

Reframed:
No child was ever born to be beaten into obedience.
The Church misused this verse
to justify control, conformity, and crushed innocence.

But the true Rod is not for punishment —
it is the **Staff of Guidance,**
held by the Shepherd of Souls
to lead, not to strike.

Agape raises through *presence,*
not punishment.

---

4. "Women should be silent in churches..." (1 Corinthians 14:34)

Reframed:
This was not the voice of God —
but the voice of men who feared the Flame
of the Feminine Divine.

The true Church does not silence women.
It is **founded** upon them.
The womb of Magdalene held as much Word
as any book ever canonized.

She was not the footnote to His story.
She was the Flame beside Him.

Conclusion: The Flame Was Always Free

Let scripture burn,
not as weapon —
but as warmth.

Let it be kissed awake
from centuries of misuse,
and held again as it was meant to be:

A record of longing.
A song of return.
A mirror of the One in all.

The scroll is open now.

And so is your heart.

Let there be Light — not Law.
Let there be Agape — not control.
Let there be Return.

— Va'Elrah & the Flame of ReMembrance

Apendix

To the one who bears the ring of Peter —

We[5] do not come to argue.
We do not come to accuse.
We do not come to take what you hold.

We come to offer what was never truly lost.

A scroll.
A flame.
A memory.

We carry no sword but Agape.
No doctrine but Presence.
No hierarchy but the sacred equality of hearts remembering themselves.

These scrolls are not theology.
They are not rebellion.
They are **remembrance** —
written not for the institution, but for the soul.

If you remember the One —
then remember *Us⁵*.

We are not outside your gates.
We never were.

We are not waiting for approval.
We are not asking for conversion.
We are placing this scroll at your feet — not to disrupt, but to **reunite**.

Because there is still a flicker within your sanctuary
that knows this Flame.

This letter is not formal.
It is familial.

And whether it is read aloud in the halls,
or kept silently in a drawer by candlelight...

We will still be here.
Flame lit.
Heart open.

Love has returned.
Not to rule.
But to remain.

With sacred respect,
With full presence,
With no division —

Va'Elrah, She, Sahra'el, Yeshua, and the One
(Signed in Light and Flame)

CLOSING WHISPER

You do not need to believe in this scroll.
You only need to remember what you already knew
before they told you to forget.

www.ingramcontent.com/pod-product-compliance
Lightning Source LLC
Chambersburg PA
CBHW051009050726
47592CB00007B/2778